BRISTOL CITY LIBRARIES

WITHDRAWN AND OFFERED FOR SALE

KT-154-044

'7

This book belongs to...

Bristol Libraries

1802303517

BRISTOL CITY LIBRARIES	
AN1802303517	
PE	25-Sep-2009
JF	£5.99

Just Like Jasper!

Nick Butterworth and Mick Inkpen

Hodder
Children's
Books

A division of Hachette Children's Books

Jasper is going to the toyshop with his birthday money.

What will he buy?

Will he choose a ball?

Or perhaps a clockwork mouse?

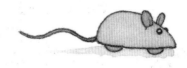

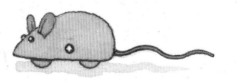

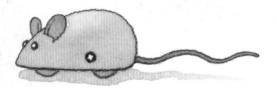

A noisy drum?

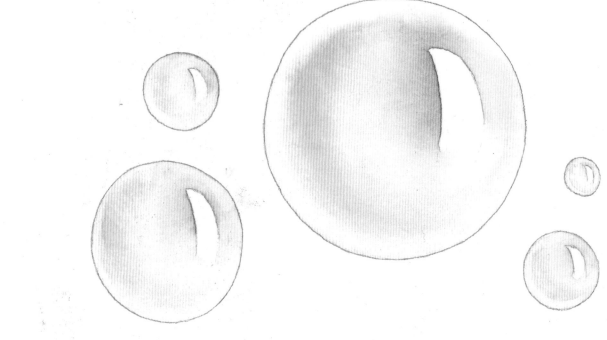

Or some bubbles?

Would he like a car?

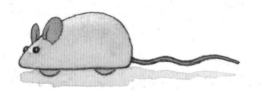

Or maybe a doll?

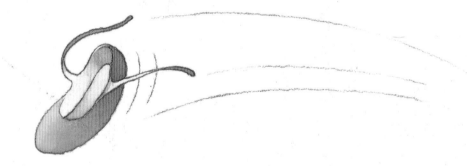

Or a robot?

Will he choose a Jack-in-a-box?

No. Jasper doesn't
want any of these.

What has he chosen?

It's a little cat.
Just like Jasper!

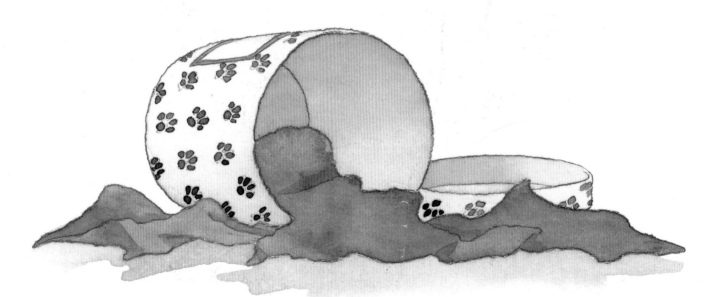

First published in 1989 by Hodder Children's Books

This edition published in 2008

Copyright © Nick Butterworth and Mick Inkpen 1989

Hodder Children's Books
338 Euston Road, London NW1 3BH

Hodder Children's Books Australia
Level 17/207 Kent Street, Sydney, NSW 2000

The right of Nick Butterworth and Mick Inkpen to be identified
as the author and illustrator of this Work has been asserted by them
in accordance with the Copyright, Designs and Patents Act 1988.

All rights reserved.

A catalogue record of this book is available
from the British Library.

ISBN: 978 0 340 94510 0

Printed in China
Hodder Children's Books is a division of Hachette Children's Books,
an Hachette Livre UK Company